MW00411689

god's breath hovering across the waters

Also by Henry Israeli

Poetry
New Messiahs
Praying to the Black Cat

As Translator
Fresco: Selected Poetry of Luljeta Lleshanaku
Child of Nature
Haywire

god's breath hovering across the waters

Henry Israeli

Four Way Books
Tribeca

Copyright © 2016 by Henry Israeli
No part of this book may be used or reproduced in any manner
without written permission except in the case of brief quotations
embodied in critical articles and reviews.

Please direct all inquiries to:
Editorial Office
Four Way Books
POB 535, Village Station
New York, NY 10014
www.fourwaybooks.com

Library of Congress Cataloging-in-Publication Data

Names: Israeli, Henry, 1967- author.
Title: god's breath hovering across the waters / Henry Israeli.
Description: New York, NY : Four Way Books, [2016]
Identifiers: LCCN 2016007105 | ISBN 9781935536765 (softcover : acid-free paper)
Classification: LCC PS3609.S66 A6 2016 | DDC 811/.6--dc23
LC record available at http://lccn.loc.gov/2016007105

This book is manufactured in the United States of America and printed on acid-free paper.

Four Way Books is a not-for-profit literary press. We are grateful for the assistance
we receive from individual donors, public arts agencies, and private foundations.

NEW YORK STATE OF OPPORTUNITY. Council on the Arts

This publication is made possible with public funds from the New York State Council on the Arts,
a state agency.

[clmp]

We are a proud member of the Community of Literary Magazines and Presses.

Distributed by University Press of New England
One Court Street, Lebanon, NH 03766

CONTENTS

Mother,
Even this crumb of life I also owe to you.

—Donald Revell

god's breath

hovering over the waters (His Master's Voice)

1.

In 1964, Arno Penzias and Robert Woodrow Wilson built an ultra-sensitive cryogenic microwave receiver, a large metallic funnel that looked like a megaphone for a demented and egomaniacal giant, and discovered an inexplicable sound they assumed had something to do with all those damn pigeons shitting on their invention. So they cleaned it up and even shot all the pigeons they could, massacred a busload of incontinent squab, yet that noise, not quite static, white and febrile and infinite, persisted. Having crossed pigeon guano off their list of potential culprits, Penzias and Wilson came up with only one reasonable explanation: they were listening to the remnants of the Big Bang.

2.

Today my mother was run over by a Volkswagen SUV
while delivering Rosh Hashanah presents to her doctors.
Today god's breath, hot and metallic, weighs 4,700 pounds.
Was all that really necessary to kill a woman with osteoporosis,
heart disease, hepatitis C, and chronic indigestion,
someone who barely weighed one hundred pounds soaking wet?

Several people who witnessed it surrounded her
like a protective shield. A woman who held her hand
until the ambulance came later said my mother
was worried the doctors wouldn't get their presents.

3.

The inside of my head is pounding.
So much wet bread stuck to its walls.
The bravest and the weakest
meet in the center of a field
and exchange numbers.
They all fall before the thresher.

A broken bottle is a thing of beauty
especially if it is green.
Where it touches the body,
the point of harvest. A murky
patina covers the aquarium
and we pretend to ignore it.

Once I was young and had accomplished
so much I could have died
with a grin on my face.
Tonight I am handcuffed
to a kewpie doll and crave
the sweet suffocation of a blackout.

4.

What can be said of the god of rats
who takes such care of the rat world
and gives them immortality in an afterlife,
a kind of rat heaven with endless sewer pipes
feeding them succulent morsels of decaying
fruit, chicken bones, a soufflé of our daily detritus,
a kind of inside out New York City in the sky?

What can be said of the god of spiders
that live in my barbecue. Don't they know their home
gets torched every week or two?

Is that the best they can do?

5.

At the airport, on my way home from shiva
I see two security guards

checking a woman's prosthetic leg.
She is seated as they hover over her,

the man and woman who moments earlier
were teasing each other about

boyfriends and girlfriends. Her stump
hangs over the edge of the chair,

and they peer inside the hollow leg
as if looking through a telescope

at the surface of the moon, a scene
that could be in a corner of a Bosch painting

depicting the end of the world.
The man turns his head, puts his ear

to the hole in the leg, and listens.

6.

Death drives a foreign car. He brings reusable bags when he goes to the grocery store. He wants everyone to know he cares. He pays his taxes on time. He exercises enough but not too much. He gives to a wide array of charities but not so much that it seems he's showing off. He keeps extra cash on the side, just in case. He hates traveling, never takes the train. Flying freaks him out. He drinks socially but never gets drunk. He wants to be liked. He cries when he watches sad films, so he never watches sad films. He enjoys the company of strangers more than that of his so-called friends and family. He has a sweet tooth. He rarely lets on what he's thinking unless pressed. He has his shirts pressed but not his pants. He has a weight problem, but there's nothing he can do about it. He makes love tenderly but has trouble sleeping afterward. He's not religious, but he is traditional. He reads the horoscopes whenever he can. He has a perverse attraction to the careless. He enjoys his down time but never takes his mind off work. He always wants to get to know you better. He wishes he had accomplished more.

7.

When he was six years old, Arno Penzias became
part of what was known as the Kindertransport—
along with 10,000 other Jewish children,
he was spirited out of Nazi Germany
and settled first in England, later
in New York City, with his parents.

When my mother was five, she was smuggled—
along with her parents—across the river that divided
Nazi-occupied Poland from Soviet-occupied Poland.
The Germans patrolling their side opened fire
and a bullet grazed her, tearing a hole in her jacket.
That day, the blessed bullet missed its mark.

8.

How much does god's breath weigh?

As much as the little diamonds
embedded on the gold hand
hanging around my daughter's neck
on a piece of yarn she cut herself.

My mother died with that hand
against her chest. Inside, a heart,
broken and stitched together
with arteries from her legs.

When I was three, my mother
was diagnosed with Hodgkin's disease.
Massive doses of radiation were beamed
toward all of her lymph nodes.

I had no idea what she was going through.
I thought all mothers wore wigs.

When I was seventeen
she suffered a heart attack,

possibly the result of the poorly focused
radiation so many years earlier.

I don't remember when
she began wearing the hand
but I hardly remember
seeing her without it.

My daughter wears it now—
the hand of god—
meant to dispel evil spirits and curses.

9.

I stand by the tracks on my way to work,
counting my good fortunes.
I count three: my wife, my children, my home.
Yet today I feel about as useful as a single chopstick.

The sun is out after a long rain
and the world smells like my mother's
hand lotion. My shadow hugs me so tightly
I can't see it, and my tongue wants no part of me.
Even my feet want to walk away.

I daydream that my mother missed a green light,
got out of her car five seconds later
and was never run over.

I blink and the dream abandons me
the way water sheds a swimmer
as he climbs the ladder.

Leaves fall around me,
the ground a ghastly yellow.

10.

Where were you, I ask.

I was there.

No, I mean, where were you?

Why are you spelling my name with a lower case g?

I've lost respect for you.

Then why are you speaking to me?

I feel as if you keep changing the subject.

I am one, one is I.

Is that supposed to make me feel better?

I don't care if you feel better. That's not my job.

What is your job, I ask.

My job is to make you fear me,
to let you know that I can snatch you up like a pickle from a jar
and finish you off in three bites,
that every moment you live is because I have decided
not to kill you, that I am fickle and jealous
and change my mind easily,
that one day you may be running some errands
whistling a ditty in your head,
and I will cut you down like a sheaf of wheat
quicker than you can blink.

Then you must be good at your job.

god blows my hair back with his hot breath,
god with a capital G.

11.

Arno Penzias once said:
    "Astronomy leads us to a unique event,
    a universe that was created
    out of nothing and delicately balanced
    to provide exactly the conditions
    required to support life.
    In the absence of an absurdly improbable accident,
    the observations of modern science seem to suggest
    an underlying, one might say,
    supernatural plan."

Dr. Penzias, with all due respect,
absurdly improbable accidents
happen all the time. How could someone
back up over a seventy-five-year-old woman
at under five miles per hour?
What is the probability
that he doesn't see her, hits her,
then continues backing up,
smashing her pelvis, rupturing a major artery?
Would anyone say it was a supernatural event?

And so, like an oblivious young man in an SUV,
can the universe simply roll along, continually expanding,
mass having compressed and then exploded,
leaving one little planet
at exactly the right distance from a sun
with exactly the right geological make up,
spinning at exactly the right speed,
covered with the precise mix of gasses,
surrounded in a protective magnetic shield,
that can generate and support life indefinitely?

Hell, yes.

12.

Nipper, the black and white mutt,
listening to "His Master's Voice,"

stares mutely into the gramophone horn.
The image of a dog

fooled into thinking that his master
is somehow at the other end

of a brass horn has captivated
people for over a century.

Nipper's master, Mark Henry Barraud,
died two years before the photograph

that inspired the painting
that inspired the logo.

Even more profound, a dog amused
by the detached ghost-voice of its master?

Except that it never happened.
The dumb mongrel was caught

gazing into the horn for no apparent reason.
Perhaps he heard his own doggy

breath echoed and amplified
back to him. Perhaps he thought

another dog, a bitch in heat, was in there.
Whatever the reason, the image and its legend

live on, while reality died a quick death.
We can't keep dogs or people from hearing

what they want to hear, believing
what they want to believe.

Evidence will always back them.
The Big Bang? god's breath?

The illogic of my mother's death?
We only have senses

with simplistic hardware (eyes, nose,
tongue, fingertips, and those conical

extensions we call ears) to help
guide us through our world—

and any abstraction we can dream up,
anything that makes our story

easier to grasp, keeps us from falling
into our own personal black holes—

which is one of millions of billions
hurtling through what we call space.

30TH STREET STATION

My chopsticks fall out at the train station,
tumble from a wrapper that depicts
the history of the chopstick along with instructions
for occidentals and an illustration
of a panda bear ecstatic about soy sauce.
A woman nods at her phone, agreeing with its text message.
I daydream of noodles, long
noodles falling into a deep white bowl.
I chase them with chopsticks before me
like a couple of horns. I'm going in for the kill.
In my mind, I'm making love to my wife
in a bowl of noodles. I've read about a new virus
that makes you do everything backwards—
walk, talk, even sleep—and I think, as I stand up
and look around me, patting my pockets to feign normalcy,
that I might have it. The conductor stares at me,
his eyes asking, *Why would you want*
to climb aboard the train you just stepped off of?

A NEBULA

A nebula is a cloud of dust, gas, and plasma
that may one day form stars and planets.
A nebula is also a cloudlike spot on the cornea.
How I ended up in Pennsylvania
I'll never fully understand.
Pennsylvania has always been a nebula
to me, a land of green John Deeres
working like synchronized swimmers
to make perfect crop circles, although—
come to think of it—my first love
was from Pennsylvania. It was 1986,
and I felt as if I were swimming in a cloud all day long.
In 964, al-Sufi spotted the Andromeda Galaxy
but did not notice the prominent Orion nebula
perhaps because of a nebula on his cornea.
It took me three months in 2004, a time
between living in one place in Pennsylvania
and another place in Pennsylvania,
to figure out my marriage was dead.
In 1964, Pablo Picasso painted his fourth
version of *Head of a Bearded Man*.
He slept with many women, sometimes even his wife.
When I moved out of the coach house
we were renting on part of a horse farm,
I grew a badass beard and dreamt

of riding a motorcycle but never did.
I came to Pennsylvania once in 1987
to break up with my girlfriend,
which I regretted for years.
It's likely I have been blind
many times in my life.
Pennsylvania is my home now.
I have married another Pennsylvanian
and she is as strong as the state is wide.
It seems I have a thing for them—Pennsylvanians.
Although it has no beard, the sky in Pennsylvania
sometimes hangs so low I want to reach up and give
a little tug to its big Amish chin.

A CANTICLE WITH DASHES OF REMORSE

The mother in the movie *Mother* would kill for her son.
Not so my mother, who, if anything went wrong,
laid blame squarely on me. If a kid hit me,
I probably deserved it. And why was I bothering her about it anyway?
And how about hitting him back? That never worked out well for me.
One kid boxed my ears and left no bruises
but a pain in my head so excruciating you'd think
he was professionally trained in torture.
A thousand of me fell into myself, like swimmers
choreographed to look like the petals of a closing flower.

                I confess that when I was six
I snuck into the house they were building next door
and painted the walls myself.
I mixed pink insulation into several cans of paint
and reached as high as a six year old could
to spread my personal vision across the newly built house.
Still, I was surprised when the police
came knocking at our door, asking to speak to my mother.
I hid in the garage, waiting to be turned in,
envisioning life behind bars with prison slop on metal trays
and clothes so baggy they practically dripped off.
But no one called for me. Not for questions or punishment.

Not a word was mentioned, but there was plenty of talk
around the neighborhood about who the vandals probably were
and what they had done.

I never told my mother,
and eventually it seemed too silly
to bring up at all. Would she even remember?
But now, for some reason, I wish I could ask her
if she protected me from the law that day
or if she just thought her little angel was incapable of the destruction
I did so easily and dutifully, with hardly any effort at all.

BRAVING THE ELEMENTS

My head is a ball of yarn
with needles poking through it at angles
making me feel like a satellite
reeling through orbit. I hear a student
discussing with her tutor what's ethically right for Susan.
What's ethically right for Susan is not necessarily
ethically right for Sara, so don't complain, Susan.
I pull a needle out of my head.
I want to civilize myself, want to
walk into a painting of snow, a white canvas
without any paint. What do we share?
A beach house with no beach? *Stay*, I say,
but I don't know whom I'm talking to.
Sara is long gone. What use is yarn to anyone?
It is not ethically right for Susan, says the tutor,
to impose her normalcy on others.
I couldn't agree more.

DARK MATTER

The last time I saw my mother was in a parking lot
but not the one she would die in.
Well, technically, she died in the hospital.
They didn't know her pelvis had been shattered,
that she was filling with her own blood,
that dark matter was both draining and drowning her.
I wanted to write a light poem about dark matter,
something about all the dark matter that makes up the vastness
of the universe. This is a dark poem, I'm sorry.

To be precise, dark matter is not dark
but closer to transparent.
It's everything that cannot be seen
but still exists in between what can.
The young man who ran over my mother
said he didn't see her. I question the truth
behind this statement. Matter exists between everything
we see, even if we don't see it.

My mother was not dark matter
the day the young man killed her.
But she is today. Sometimes I see her
in the spaces that emit no light or color or radiation—
but I am no sentimentalist. It's not her spirit I sense,

it's her absence—dark matter
that cannot be detected by any instrument,
nor seen by any eye, not even heard.
But as hard as it is to imagine,
I feel the not being of her
as certainly as I feel the gravity
that keeps me from floating away—
or the gravity that keeps me from
writing a light poem about dark matter.

THE MOTHER'S SONG

The mother's song is
        the sound of the boot
compressing the snow
        the sound of the bayonet
stabbing a bale of hay
        the sound of a gunshot
behind the barn
        the sound of a spade
edging into dry earth
        the sound of a prayer
muttered by the doomed
        penitent hiding behind
a curtain his mouth
        taped shut his thumbs
cut off and a hole in
        his throat through which
a thrush reaches out
        a worm in its beak
blind and twisted
        as an ampersand
a child practiced
        over and over
in a black book
        as punishment for

daring to imagine
    the mother's song
that's written on torn
    white wings from
the other side
    of understanding
where everything
    has a way of breathing
and everything
    is as wondrous as
waking up in rags
    on a forest floor
realizing that no one
    survived not even
those who live—

THE SEQUEL

In the next chapter
I feel the blood stop cold in my body
and reverse its course.
Is this a disease, slipped into me
like a counterfeit bill into a cash register,
or is it my feeble attempt to feel something
again, that wheedling sensation
that something vital has shifted,
question marks spun round as in Spanish text?
My baby girl is growing up, her monsters
becoming real. My wife unpacks box
after box like a mad magician. And I am trying
to make sense of my life through words,
painstakingly unwrapping each one
and hammering it to paper.
I wouldn't wish this on a dog.
In the next chapter,
branches overgrow my house
and a horde of spiders wraps it,
lifts it off the ground. This is a bad idea
for all of us, even the spiders.
When camping, my daughter wakes me at dawn to kill one.
She doesn't realize the futility in this.
Nature is slowly killing us, I want to explain,

and all monsters are real.
My wife redecorates in her mind. I walk
around the block and imagine it's a different block
each time. I dig for truffles
in my sleep.

THEORY OF THE BIG BANG

1.

Picture everything that exists
not just on this planet
but in the universe,
once densely compacted
into one solid mass

then exploding outward
                              its particles
               becoming the cosmos
               planets, gases
                              and debris between them.

Then, instead of slowing down
                    like shrapnel in an explosion,
picture the countless shards of the universe
               speeding up.

2.

Funny how each day seems to move
　　　　more quickly than the last. Funny how
when someone walks in front or behind
　　　　a moving car I can picture my mother
run over in slow motion as if her feet are stuck
　　　　in hot tar. Funny how the car first tips her
over and then moves across her hips
　　　　crushing her pelvis, severing the femoral artery.
Funny how as I lunge toward her,
　　　　I move in slow motion, too, my mouth open
as someone drowning struggles to the surface
　　　　with eternal darkness in his mouth.
Funny how all I can do once I reach her
　　　　is cradle her head in my arms the way
she once cradled my soft lolling skull in hers,
　　　　a perverse parody of birth, her uterus
flattened, me crying out *mama mama*,
　　　　a crowd of spectators forming a black curtain
closing around us, the sunshine white
　　　　and blinding as the imagined afterlife.

3.

Life without a body,
a brain without the senses . . .

I am asking you to imagine the unimaginable—
      to see the planets in other solar systems

without a telescope, without eyes,
                          without reason
or intelligence or perception, without so much as
the nerve
      impulse
of an oyster or the light seeking feelers
      of the blindly creeping morning glory.

                      Without without.

Remember, the Earth slowly moves
toward the sun and will one day be swallowed
whole by her bosom.

We live day to day as if watching
ourselves being watched
                              from far away,

a distance farther than we can ever conceive of
and therefore can never truly fathom

        that we are already dead.

THIS POEM WILL NOT DIE, SO I BEAT IT SENSELESS

It's as if a sniper has been hovering
over me somewhere, on a bridge perhaps,

and picking off people one by one.
What message is he sending? Why can't he

communicate like a mensch (spellcheck suggests *menace*)?
My daughter wants to see *Romeo and Juliet*.

I won't let her. Too much death.
Too much death in this life, for that matter,

one for each of us—the odds of being born
are so slim—of dying, well, it's 1:1.

I used to know so many suicides;
now the deaths around me are earned

the hard way—unexpectedly, on no one's terms.
First my mother, swift and brutal,

then our neighbor who made
peanut brittle for our daughters

collapsed one night while brushing her hair,
then my daughter's allergist,

one day they told me he was gone.
Death, you are a menace (spellcheck suggests *mensch*).

THE GREAT SOVIET SPACE DOG EXPERIMENT

1.

Nipper, the rascal mutt of RCA
fame, forever gazing into

a cylinder phonograph
with an idiotic tilt of his head,

never made it into orbit,
but Dezik the Soviet space dog did

along with his floozy Tsygan.
He cheated on her with Lisa,

and they died in what might be
the most romantic death in history—

paw-to-paw above Stalin's Georgia.
Another Lisa paired up with a bitch

named Ryzhik, and they made it
a hundred kilometers into suborbital

space without a hitch, the first
and only all-female space flight.

Smalaya managed to run away—
not every dog is suited for fame—

as did Bolik, who was never found,
making his mark in history

as the space dogs' biggest mystery.
Kruschev beat a shoe against

his desk for days, but no dog came
running, tail a-wagging, tongue agog.

Damka and Krasavka landed safely
but not so Bars and Lisichka,

burned to a crisp for mother Russia.
Not much luckier was Laika,

first dog to reach orbit. Like many
Soviets, she died of melancholia,

her petrified mug immortalized
on a forty ruble stamp. Pchyolka

and Mushka were blown to specks.
Many said it rained dogs all day long

over Siberia. They said it without irony.
Children looked skyward with mouths

open to get a taste of galactic glory.
Veterok and Ugolyok spent a record

twenty-two days in space, their floppy
ears flung high in zero gravity.

Their flight marked the end of
the great Soviet space dog experiment

though no one celebrates
their accomplishment any longer.

Since then there've been monkeys, mice,
turtles, fruit flies, silkworms, even a cat—

forbid the thought. Disappointments all.
Stalin and Kruschev had it right—

they knew dogs were made for flight.

2.

Kruschev said, "Our dogs are cosmonauts,
your dogs are assholes." And he's right.

Our dogs sit, lie, heel, and lift their paws.
Their dogs fly in rocket ships!

Our dogs shit on freshly mowed lawns.
Their dogs' turds float in zero gravity

like gloomy thought bubbles.
Our dogs beg for scraps at our feet.

Their dogs catch kibble in midair.
Our dogs bark when the neighbors barbecue.

When their dogs bark, the sound
travels deep into the galaxy.

Our dogs hump grandmas' legs,
their furry pelvises gyrating over

white anti-embolism stockings.
Their dogs fuck each other at angles

only dreamt up in the Kama Sutra.
Our dumb dogs chase their own tails,

spinning themselves into dizzying circles
until they collapse, retching.

Their dogs win the space race.
How can one compare the two?

Kruschev said, "One day we will bury you."
Of course, what he meant was,

"One day our dogs will bury you,
and on another day they will dig you up,

gnaw on your bones, lick them
clean, and then bury you again."

WHAT OF THE FLEA

Wherein could this flea guilty be ...
—John Donne

What of the flea in its canine kingdom,
king of dung and blood and foul, fleshly deeds?
If you want to get down and dirty, if you want to know life
in its rawest, most godless, carnal cornucopia, go ask the flea
that gazes up at you, that sees you for what you are,
alien life on a distant planet. The flea hunched
in its diver's pose, tracks your dog's eye,
moon in its perpetual midnight. Hungering so pitilessly,
it will burrow through its dead brethren
to reach a patch of warm flesh and sip a drop
of the divine mutt's elixir. It has no conscience, no fear.
It spends so much of its existence in a larval state
that dying is nothing but another chrysalis, a rebirth.
How sick and sad its life, how much it wants you
to feel the echo of its misery, that it bites without discretion,
bites and breeds and burrows amid feces and scraps
wilting off the skin like white dahlias in snow.
The flea is the opposite of god, it makes supper of dog,
it lives on blood and blood alone, and when its furry world dies
the flea abandons it without a second thought, migrates
to another, to love it with the same blasé perversion,
to love it fully as only a flea can, till kingdom come, till hallowed be
and hallelujah and amen all rolled into one,
one awful flea, that sucks and sucks, guiltless and guilty.

DEPRAVED COGITATION

In the movie, two teenage boys find a naked zombie woman
tied to a table, and one decides to keep her as a kind of girlfriend.
Don't laugh. Stranger things have happened.
Someone shot Archduke Ferdinand,
a second rate monarch of a third rate nation,
and that started a world war, for Christ's sake.
In my first grade class, a boy shit his pants
and even though we could all smell it,
the teacher never even noticed.
Life is full of odd events that lead to odder
circumstances. You're not supposed to ask
who tied the zombie woman to the table
in the middle of an abandoned insane asylum,
or what exactly an Archduke does,
or what kind of numbskulls
are in charge of your children eight hours a day.
Just go with it, or learn the art of augury,
invest in the right tenements,
have a smoke in a haystack,
or better yet, think of the fish served in China,
cooked yet still alive, heart beating,
eyes sad and pleading for mercy, tail flicking
back and forth as you reach out with your chopsticks,
then question your motives. Ask yourself, are you really

as good a person as you thought you were?
You are stubborn, you are greedy,
you are horny, and full of disgust and resentment for nearly everyone.
You wind a toy up until the spring breaks,
you kill ladybugs that fly into your house,
you wear colors and patterns that make people dizzy.
The boys in the movie get their comeuppance
in a dazzling display of gore and carnage.
Gavrilo Princip died in prison, a painful death by tuberculosis.
The boy in my first grade class grew up
to be a certified public accountant.
And I, even after becoming an orphan at forty-two—
got off easy. Easy as pie.
True enough. But everyone has a zombie tied up
in the basement. And one day it will bite
someone you love, and then she will be a zombie,
slowly rotting as you bring her gifts,
brush her hair, rub cream on her dry, brittle skin,
and make sweet, sweet love to her.

THE GARDEN OF EARTHLY DELIGHTS

I love the little buns they sell in Chinatown,
the white ones, steamy hot and a little sticky,
with surprise meats inside.
You never know what you'll get!
I can't understand why everyone doesn't eat this way.
Clearly Hieronymus Bosch is not god.
Nor, unfortunately, is any Dutchman.
Surely god is a Spaniard
who lets emotions get the better of him.
Weeds will always overgrow the garden
and a wheelchair always wins the race.
So too do I love the tension the moment after
the television is turned on, before the picture appears,
a kind of nocturnal chaos of sound
and vision you could read like tea leaves
if only it weren't sucked into the vortex
of logic and meaning so quickly:
some asshole selling cars or computers,
selling immortality in a microchip.
I envy those who've had shock treatment. Imagine
the wonders they've seen. Imagine taking every memory
and running it through the spin cycle. Imagine
sweeping clean your karmic portico with 450 volts.
What ever happened to *deliverance?*

No one mentions it anymore, no one gives a fuck.
Two soldiers died today,
blown apart in Mesopotamia, the cradle of civilization,
while I reject two artichokes in the produce section of Superfresh.
The devil, wherever he is, snuffs out
the candle on his bedside table, and whacks off
to dreams of a burnt out cradle.

PERSONAL JESUS

I want to see your face, not just your words,
but I know I will be disappointed.
What kind of a face could you have
that would not disappoint?
I made squash soup the other day.
It was too bitter so I added more sugar,
then too sweet so I added more salt,
then too salty so I threw up my hands
and asked you what to do.
Your face swirled briefly in the broth
before sinking back to the bottom of the pot
like a species of crab that only comes to the surface
to breathe once a month.
In that moment you gave me that look that says *fuck it*
so I did nothing and the soup was pretty good
although nothing to write home about.
When I backpacked through Europe
long before most people knew about the Internet,
I wrote home about a lot of things
although none of them so important
that I *had to* write home about them.
I kissed any girl I could, and probably
would have written home about that
if I had actually written home about the things

that mattered most to me. I fell into the face
of any girl who would let me. I thought
this is how it's done: you just fall into their faces.
Some let me. Some didn't. It didn't matter much.
Was I looking for you in their faces?
No, my eyes were closed.
Was I looking for you in the dark swirl
behind my eyelids? In the breasts I kissed?
The thighs I ran my fingers along?
Your naked body pulled off the cross
and washed by Mary Magdalene?
All the biblical figures, from the New and Old Testament,
imagined by painters with the wind blowing the clothes
off their backs, were so frustrated
because they longed to see your face.
They look like they could fuck each other
over. I want to see your face now
but I never will. I know your secret.
You have no face, no more than
a lake has a face, or a bowl of soup,
and it's best that way.

MISSING CHILDREN

When a parent dies, the child goes
missing, and takes on the dead dim glow
of those computer-aged faces.

And when the missing child laughs
flashlights slash the darkness
and boots plod through the marsh.

"I think I've found him," someone cries out.
But no, it is only a log, a log with a boot
on one limb, a mitten on another.

A BOUQUET OF KNIVES

When I bend down to smell them
I get an eerie feeling that I've done this before
and it came to a sorry end.
What drives me to lower my bucket into the well
again, like the bird that keeps flying into the window
above my desk? He smacks himself silly, darts off,
and does the same thing the next day.
Stop for a second, bird, and think about
what idiot god designed you for such an absurd,
redundant purpose? What kind of a jerk
would garner pleasure from your suffering?
Can't you do something else compulsively,
something more self-serving? Like building nests
for all the lazy birds? But look at me.
I'm talking to a bird. I'm asking it questions
over and over as if it might look down from my window
and tweet, "This is what I do.
What do you do, you boob?" He'd have a point.
We all have to fashion a purpose
out of the mundane things that occupy our
attention. I, for instance, am a knife picker.
I like the sharp ones with the ivory handles best.
I arrange them in a tall clear vase

with just enough water to keep them fresh.
They smell so good I just have to
bend down and take a deep whiff
even if it means losing face.

THE BOOK OF FIXED STARS

In place of sleep, a long, sedulous sigh.
In place of comfort, a handful of fish entrails.
In place of slaughter, a gurgling, wet orifice.
What takes the place of joy, al-Sufi asks,
but no one volunteers. Al-Sufi observes
the bloody gash of the ecliptic plane,
the path on which the pilgrim sun travels yearly,
and thinks, *when the prophet has a tantrum*
he is sent to his room where he cuts himself.
Al-Sufi contemplates the large Magellanic Cloud
while his patron, the Emir, vanquishes neighboring Mesopotamia.
When he lays his head on an astrolabe, he dreams
of a galaxy trapped inside a dog's mouth
which the dog won't let go of until a gramophone
is placed next to him. When he releases it,
it spins down the tornado-shaped cone,
emerging in the form of a song.
So that's what dogs are for, he notes.
When, the next day, he recalls his dream,
the cat looks at him skeptically, which, to be fair,
is how the cat always looks at him.

BRAINDEAD

I thrash around all night, my thoughts escaping any way they can.
I walk to the sink to wash my face but when I look in the mirror
I see no expression at all. This disturbs me to no end, but doesn't show.
I brush my teeth, shower, dress, but still nothing. I drive quickly, then slowly,
hoping to jolt something inside me. People honk and make rude gestures
for clearly they've never seen anyone as thoughtless.
Am I a new phenomenon that warrants careful study?
Could I donate myself to science? Would they appreciate me
or would I become as unimportant as a toothpick left idly in the corner of the lab?
As I teach English 101, my students raise their hands to answer questions,
and sometimes they laugh at an offhand remark about an essay we're reading.
They have no idea I'm not thinking at all. When I come home I wonder:
should I look for my thoughts, as if somehow I could coax them back?
Should I call out, *sooeey*, like the pig farmers in Iowa? A fool's errand, I know—
thoughts never return to their birthplace. They'd rather die
than be subjected to that prison again. And who can blame them?
I pour a drink and spread out across the lawn furniture, stare up at the sky.
I see two white butterflies bumping into each other, flying apart,
then knocking into each other again. Are they doing what I think they are?
Or are they are just exchanging little secrets, where to find
the juiciest flowers and so on? Or perhaps they are trying to lose each other,
to be rid of an all too familiar company, but some morbid fascination
compels them to try it again, for old time's sake, just give it one last try.

MONUMENTS

Twenty-five years after their divorce
my father and mother are back together—
just a stone's throw away, literally.
One happy neighborhood—quiet, at last.
No fighting this time around.
If death were sleep, their dreams might mingle—
they might give it another try, not fuck it up this time.
A child of divorce never stops fantasizing,
putting his parents back together like empty-faced dolls
at a plastic dinner table. Twenty-five years later
are they finally at peace with one another?
Did resentment and anger die with them?
Or will they fight it out with maggots?
I want to walk between their gravestones
in the winter, after a light snow
so that my boot prints stitch them together—
then I can write a dumb poem with that image.
In this way, too, I write them together
for the first time. My memories of them
make me itch in places I can't reach—
but on the page, as in the cemetery,
they live joined in a language
they learned as immigrants in their late twenties,

the letters like rows of tombstones.
I imagine my mother beneath one of them,
my father beneath another,
both wrapped in prayer shawls,
their faces looking up into my eyes.

MESOPOTAMIA, MESOPOTAMIA
OR, THE WAR ON TERROR

I am in love with fire
and shrapnel and flesh
burned clean off the bone.

I am in love with stars
that cleave to helmets
like grief to the grieving.

My voice is a lathe
shaving ambiguity
to a shiny sterling bullet.

The gates open, I let hunger in.
The gates open, I let anger out.
A porcelain wind thickens.

If violence were my edict,
I would gleam with its beauty.
I would know no reason.

If I knew how to sing
I would sing of treason.

THE HARROWING BUSINESS OF LOSS

The way the dog looks
when she can't find you.

The way branches sag
in summer's drought.

How the song's last lingering note
begs for silence.

The wooded scent detached
forever from the almond.

Searching out the dead
nightly in my dreams,

I am in the business of loss,
well practiced from birth,

my job, vocation, hobby, fad—
posting losses.

*

Remember how I cried
when my mother

left me at nursery school?
Remember how heart-

broken I was?
I would come to know

that one day she would
leave me for good

that loss was an occupation
I could handle

with humble acumen.
Yes, she was, I nod

at the many faces,
familiar and unfamiliar

offering condolences
between bites of egg

salad sandwiches,
my face like

the crumpled white
napkins in their hands.

*

Who are you?
I don't know.

Who are you?
I don't know.

The question is
are you comfortable

not knowing?
Do you lose yourself

when you lose
those you love

or do you find yourself
becoming more yourself?

It is hard to admit
that the less I have

the more I am,
that loss, like memory,

accumulates,
calcifies within me.

*

The bullet is a lonely thing.
It has no meaning without

its other. It is a question
waiting to be answered.

I am a bullet moving
farther from my mother

like matter fanning out
from the Big Bang,

velocity increasing,
so much behind, so much

ahead, metallic gleaming,
rotating clockwise,

the better to embed
into the waiting target.

*

Stopwatch with little pink cows
at each point of the cross,

two wristwatches, gold bracelets,
some earrings, a gold ring

with three diamonds
my grandfather wore,

a pearl necklace, the key
to her apartment chained

to a fat brass boot, fistfuls
of costume jewelry, and

the smell of her
clinging to all of it.

*

What is a man without a mother?
The creams and perfumes

mix with the scent of engine oil.
My eyes, two small stones.

When I kneel at her tombstone
they drop to the ground.

I'VE NEVER SEEN MY MOTHER DRUNK

I've falsified the morning with a bucket
of quivering shad, traded in the nocturnal music
of the solanaceae for a pint of river sludge,
torn the sleeves off my coat to make the garden vole
feel less awkward, cheated at ice climbing
by licking my way to the snow-capped wonders
of the Uramba Bahía Málaga National Nature Park,
but god help me, I have never seen my mother drunk.
I'll admit I've seen her looking strung out,
her head in her hands, screaming *why me* at the floor,
stumbling through the house as if she'd polished
off a bottle of rum back at the pirate ship.
I'll admit she looked up at me, her face
a cocktail party of pity and spite, her eyes
unable to face the same direction, her hands fluttering
like walrus fins at her side. But I swear I've never seen her drunk.
I envy the sons of alcoholic mothers for they have seen
the holy grail in the form of an open-mouthed
snore, in the sound of a snot-filled scream,
in a foot tripping over its sister foot, in rows of
empty bottles and rotting lime skins. Blessed are they,
who cry themselves to sleep
with the memory of shattering glass.

SWING

Once I pushed my daughter on this swing. Then
she learned to swing herself. Then the urge to swing
diminished—we both stopped pushing.
Now when I push the swing, emptiness
pushes back, the child she once was, a ghost child.
My own childhood, a ghost childhood.
My mother never pushed a swing. It wasn't
her style to push a child in any way. With every blast
of radiation therapy, she retreated more deeply into
the ghost of herself. Once childhood is shed,
a long slow skinning that aches the way a phantom limb aches,
it can drive you to lunacy, the echo of colors
bleeding out to gray. This swing swings,
pushed by no one. Laughter brined
in autumn's breeze stopped years ago
although it took me this long to know.

THEORY OF EVOLUTION

Everybody wanted a Volkswagen.
Everybody loved a Volkswagen.

Hitler demanded a Volkswagen,
a car for everybody (or anybody

who was worthy of a body)
and the *Deutsche Arbeitsfront*,

also created by Hitler, obliged.
Hitler loved the Volkswagen.

Everybody loved Hitler.
Hitler was a Volkswagen,

small and compact, full of
simple ideas everyone could grasp.

Ushered into power with one-third
of the vote, Hitler soon became

Germany's most beloved leader.
Ein Volk, ein Reich, ein Führer.

Everybody wanted a Hitler.
Everybody loved a Hitler.

Who wouldn't worship a broom
that could sweep away

all of life's detritus—
the Treaty of Versailles,

two eyes for an eye,
Jews, Gypsies, and Communist spies.

Germany created a Hitler,
and in turn, Hitler created

a Germany he could embrace
without flinching.

*

Here is a child's story
in small, compact form:

Hitler gave all the Jews stars,
but the Jews did not feel special.

They felt the opposite of special.
They felt the dirt beneath their feet

reaching up for their bones.
They felt the dreadful weight

of the world's silence,
the birth of loneliness.

My five-year-old mother
hardly knew she was a Jew.

Her parents snatched her up
and ran from the Reich

crossing the Molotov-Ribbentrop line
into Stalin's cold, dank night.

*

Everybody loved Stalin.
They had no choice.

They slid down the barrels of Tokarevs
to give his mustache wet kisses.

He pinched their cheeks
until they cried *Uncle, dear Uncle.*

They loved him so much
they worked themselves dead.

They fell, still and bloodless,
like branches of frozen larch

on the Siberian steppes.
After the war, my mother moved

back to Poland, but Poland
was a burning lake.

Nobody loved Poland,
not even the Poles.

Germany had set it on fire
and blasted it full of holes.

Warsaw looked clean as the moon
with a face freshly scrubbed

by embers and ash. Corpses
smoldered in her eyes for years.

*

Back in Deutschland,
Volkswagen and Bayer spat out

perfect little capsules for the masses,
one for the inside, one for the out.

Ein Volk, Ein Reich . . . well, not quite—
the war was over for the Krauts,

and, of course, capitalism won out.
Everybody still loved a Volkswagen.

My mother moved to Canada in '58
but never wanted a Volkswagen.

Fifty-one years later
in her doctor's parking lot,

a Volkswagen
would do her in for good,

its great Prussian bulk,
her small Jewess body,

panzer versus cavalry,
nothing spared.

     *

Deutsche Arbeitsfront's logo
used to be a black swastika

inside a black multi-pronged gear
against a blood-red backdrop—

mannish and beefy as a bootprint
stomped into a corpse.

The Volkswagen logo today
is less controversial—

a small V atop a big W,
stressing the *wagen*,

not the *volks* (*ein volk...*)—
a chrome dragonfly resting

its silver wings on the hood
of a car before lifting off

on its flight back to the fatherland.
In the celebrated "Theory of Evolution"

ad campaign, five rows of three
identical Beetles, each representing

a different year's model, stack up
neatly along a black and white page.

The message: the world changes,
but Volkswagen remains the same,

defying the edicts of evolution,
impervious to each passing decade—

for which Adolf Hitler, *Führer und
Reichskanzler*, is given little credit—

the same charming, timeless creation,
compact, tidy, and efficient.

TIME AND SPACE

I watch my mother
on an endless loop
of Super 8 from 1969,
her legs turned to the side
as she sits on the grass
with a bouffant that rests
like a black tower on her
head and her children
running to and from her
saying something inaudible
as she barely looks
at them—a planet fixed
in the eye of the camera
about to stamp her place
in time and space.

for Bianca
1934-2009

ACKNOWLEDGMENTS:

I would like to thank the superb editors of the following journals where versions of many of these poems first appeared: *American Poetry Review, Boston Review, descant, failbetter, Harvard Review, The Literary Review, Manits, Map Literary, Per Contra, Smartish Pace,* and *Zócalo Public Square.*

"Depraved Cogitation" was reprinted in the anthology *Dead and Undead Poems: Zombies, Ghosts, Vampires and Devils* (Everyman Library, 2014).

Thank you from the bottom of my heart, Sima Rabinowitz and the Yeshiva University Museum, for inviting me to take part in the *Writers on View* project, an opportunity that could not have come at a better time. My work with you was crucial not only artistically, but as a means for me to heal after my mother's sudden and tragic death. Much appreciation to Ben Rubin whose sound sculpture of the same name inspired me to write the title poem. This book wouldn't exist without you.

Thank you, Sarah Blake, Matthew Lippman, Harriet Levin, Timothy Liu, Lisa Sewell, and Gerald Stern for advice and encouragement at various stages of this book's evolution. Your intelligence and care with my work was crucial.

Thank you to Martha Rhodes for your continued faith in my work. Many thanks as well to Ryan Murphy and Bridget Bell for your astute editing skills, and thanks as well to the entire staff of Four Way Books for the care and dedication put into bringing this labor of love to fruition.

And thank you always and forever to my wife, Danielle, for the love and support you give me in every facet of my life each and every day.

Henry Israeli's poetry collections include *New Messiahs* (Four Way Books: 2002), and *Praying to the Black Cat* (Del Sol: 2010). He is also the translator of three books by Albanian poet Luljeta Lleshanaku. He has been awarded fellowship grants from the National Endowment for the Arts, Canada Council on the Arts, and elsewhere. His poetry and translations have appeared in numerous journals including *American Poetry Review, Boston Review, Harvard Review, The Iowa Review, The Literary Review,* and *Tin House,* as well as several anthologies. Henry Israeli is also the founder and editor of Saturnalia Books (saturnaliabooks.com). He is Associate Professor of English and Associate Director of the Certificate in Writing & Publishing Program at Drexel University in Philadelphia. You can follow him at henryisraeli.com.

Publication of this book was made possible by grants and donations. We are also grateful to those individuals who participated in our 2015 Build a Book Program. They are:

Jan Bender-Zanoni, Betsy Bonner, Deirdre Brill, Carla & Stephen Carlson,Liza Charlesworth, Catherine Degraw & Michael Connor, Greg Egan, Martha Webster & Robert Fuentes, Anthony Guetti, Hermann Hesse, Deming Holleran, Joy Jones, Katie Childs & Josh Kalscheur, Michelle King, David Lee, Howard Levy, Jillian Lewis, Juliana Lewis, Owen Lewis, Alice St. Claire Long & David Long, Catherine McArthur, Nathan McClain,Carolyn Murdoch, Tracey Orick, Kathleen Ossip, Eileen Pollack, BarbaraPreminger, Vinode Ramgopal, Roni Schotter, Soraya Shalforoosh, Marjorie& Lew Tesser, David Tze, Abby Wender, and Leah Nanako Winkler.